Gerald Scarfe

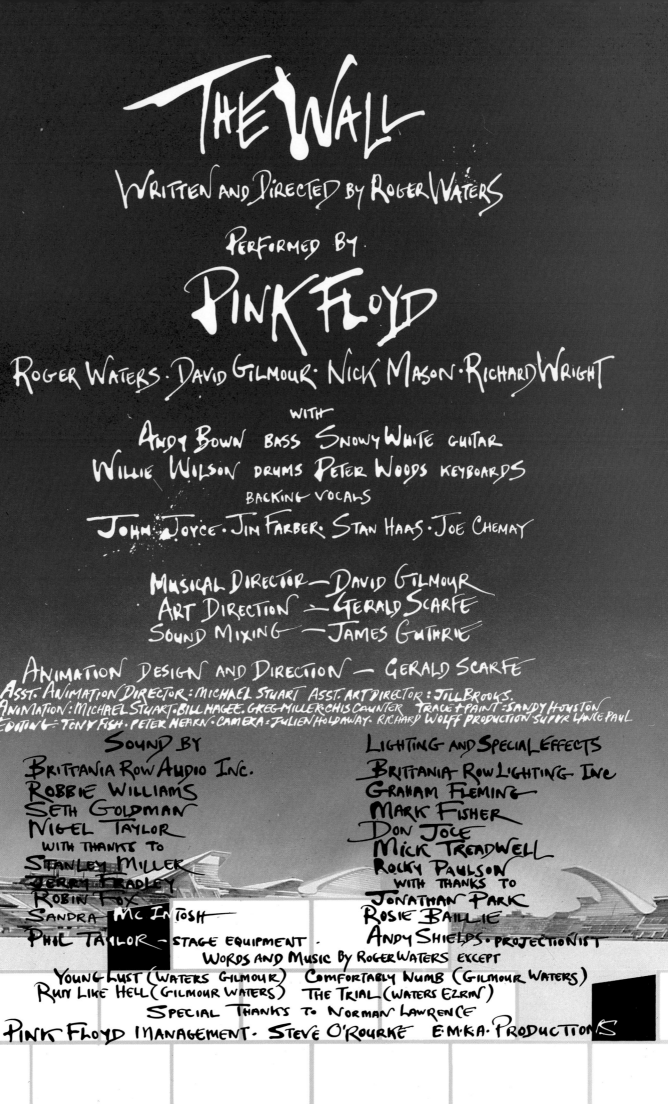

THE WALL

WRITTEN AND DIRECTED BY ROGER WATERS

PERFORMED BY

PINK FLOYD

ROGER WATERS · DAVID GILMOUR · NICK MASON · RICHARD WRIGHT

WITH

ANDY BOWN BASS SNOWY WHITE GUITAR
WILLIE WILSON DRUMS PETER WOODS KEYBOARDS
BACKING VOCALS
JOHN JOYCE · JIM FARBER · STAN HAAS · JOE CHEMAY

MUSICAL DIRECTOR — DAVID GILMOUR
ART DIRECTION — GERALD SCARFE
SOUND MIXING — JAMES GUTHRIE

ANIMATION DESIGN AND DIRECTION — GERALD SCARFE
ASST. ANIMATION DIRECTOR : MICHAEL STUART ASST. ART DIRECTOR : JILL BROOKS.
ANIMATION : MICHAEL STUART · BILL HAGEE · GREG MILLER · CHRIS CAUNTER TRACE & PAINT : SANDY HOUSTON
EDITING : TONY FISH · PETER HEARN · CAMERA : JULIEN HOLDAWAY · RICHARD WOLFF PRODUCTION SUPVR LANCE PAUL

SOUND BY	LIGHTING AND SPECIAL EFFECTS
BRITTANIA ROW AUDIO INC.	BRITTANIA ROW LIGHTING INC
ROBBIE WILLIAMS	GRAHAM FLEMING
SETH GOLDMAN	MARK FISHER
NIGEL TAYLOR	DON JOLE
WITH THANKS TO	MICK TREADWELL
STANLEY MILLER	ROCKY PAULSON
JERRY BRADLEY	WITH THANKS TO
ROBIN FOX	JONATHAN PARK
SANDRA MC INTOSH	ROSIE BAILLIE
PHIL TAYLOR — STAGE EQUIPMENT	ANDY SHIELDS · PROJECTIONIST

WORDS AND MUSIC BY ROGER WATERS EXCEPT
YOUNG LUST (WATERS GILMOUR) COMFORTABLY NUMB (GILMOUR WATERS)
RUN LIKE HELL (GILMOUR WATERS) THE TRIAL (WATERS EZRIN)
SPECIAL THANKS TO NORMAN LAWRENCE
PINK FLOYD MANAGEMENT · STEVE O'ROURKE E·M·K·A· PRODUCTIONS

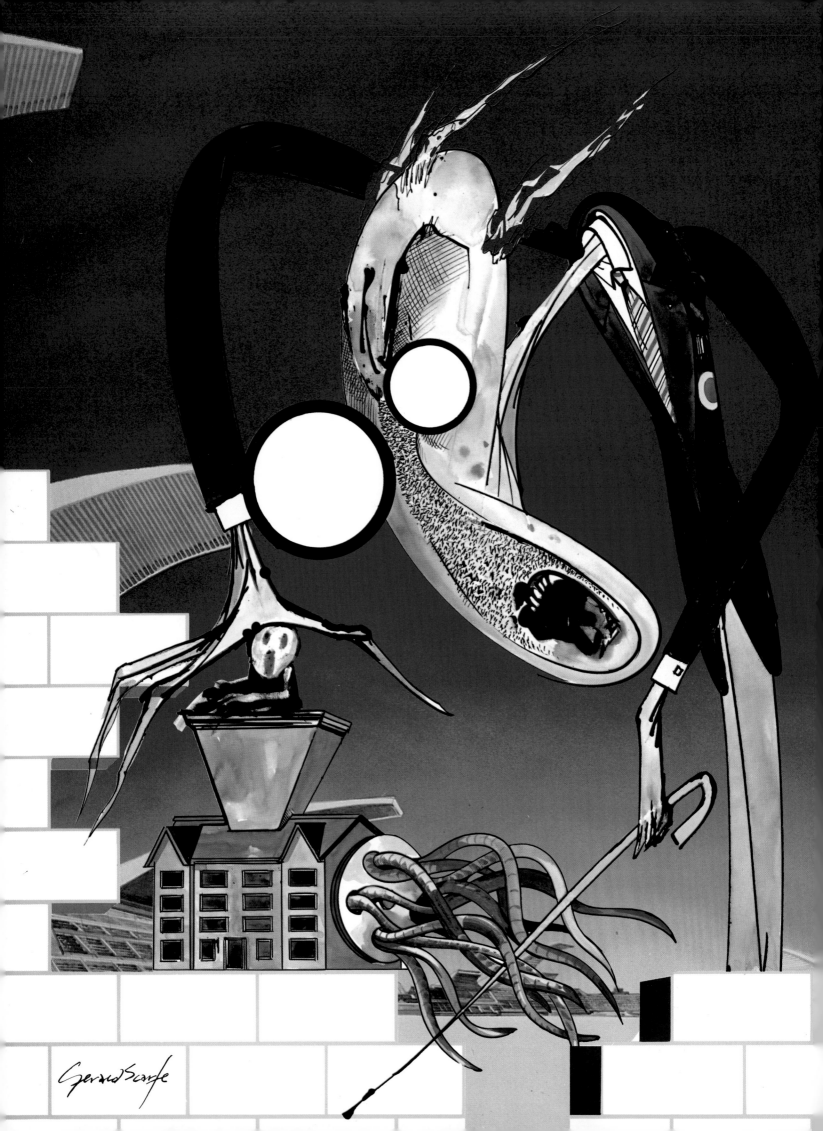

Gerald Scarfe

In the Flesh?

So ya
Thought ya
Might like to go to the show
To feel the warm thrill of confusion
That space cadet glow
Tell me is something eluding you sunshine?
Is this not what you expected to see?
If you'd like to find out whats behind these cold eyes?
You'll just have to claw your way through the
Disguise

The Thin Ice

Mamma loves her baby
And daddy loves you too
And the sea may look warm to you babe
And the sky may look blue
But Ooooh babe
Ooooh baby blue
Ooooh babe
If you should go skating
On the thin ice of modern life
Dragging behind you the silent reproach
Of a million tear stained eyes
Don't be surprised, when a crack in the ice
Appears under your feet
You slip out of your depth and out of your mind
With your fear flowing out behind you
As you claw the thin ice

Another Brick in the Wall. part 1.

Daddys flown across the ocean
Leaving just a memory
A snap shot in the family album
Daddy what else did you leave for me
Daddy what'd 'ya leave behind for me
All in all it was just a brick in the wall
All in all it was all just bricks in the wall

The Happiest Days of our Lives

When we grew up and went to school
There were certain teachers who would
Hurt the children anyway they could
By pouring their derision
Upon anything we did
And exposing every weakness
However carefully hidden by the kids
But in the town it was well known
When they got home at night, their fat and
Psychopathic wives would thrash them
Within inches of their lives

Another Brick in the Wall part 2

We don't need no education
We don't need no thought control
No dark sarcasm in the classroom
Teachers leave the kids alone,
Hey teacher leave us kids alone
All in all its just another brick in the wall
All in all you're just another brick in the wall

Mother

Mother do you think they'll drop the bomb
Mother do you think they'll like the song
Mother do you think they'll try to break my balls
Mother should I build a wall
Mother should I run for president
Mother should I trust the government
Mother will they put me in the firing line
Mother am I really dying.
Hush now baby don't you cry
Mama's gonna make all of your
Nightmares come true
Mama's gonna put all of her fears into you
mamas gonna keep you right here
Under her wing
She won't let you fly but she might let you sing
Mama will keep baby cosy and warm
Ooooh Babe Ooooh Babe Ooooh Babe
Of course Mam'll help build the wall

Mother do you think she's good enough for me
Mother do you think she's dangerous to me
Mother will she tear your little boy apart
Mother will she break my heart.

Hush now baby, baby don't you cry
mama's gonna check out all your girl friends for you
Mama won't let anyone dirty get through
Mama's gonna wait up till you come in
Mama will always find out where
You've been
Mama's gonna keep you healthy and clean
Ooooh Babe Ooooh Babe Ooooh Babe
You'll always be a baby to me
Mother, did it need to be so high.

Gerald Scarfe

Goodbye Blue Sky

Ooooooooooooooooooooh
Did you see the frightened ones
Did you hear the falling bombs
Did you ever wonder
Why we had to run for shelter
When the promise of a brave new world
Unfurled beneath a clear blue sky
Ooooooooooooooooooooh
Did you see the frightened ones
Did you hear the falling bombs
The flames are all long gone
But the pain lingers on
Goodbye Blue Sky
Goodbye Blue Sky
Goodbye

Empty Spaces / What shall we do now?

What shall we use to fill the empty
Spaces where we used to talk
How shall I fill the final places
How shall I complete the wall

Shall we buy a new guitar
Shall we drive a more powerful car
Shall we work straight through the night
Shall we get into fights
Leave the lights on
Drop bombs
Do tours of the east
Contract diseases
Bury bones
Break up homes
Send flowers by phone
Take to drink
Go to shrinks
Give up meat
Rarely sleep
Keep people as pets
Train dogs
Race rats
Fill the attic with cash
Bury treasure
Store up leisure
But never relax at all
With our backs to the wall

Outside the Wall

All alone, or in twos
The ones who really love you
Walk up and down outside the wall
Some hand in hand
Some gathering together in bands
The bleeding hearts and artists
Make their stand
And when they've given you their all
Some stagger and fall, after all its not easy
Banging your heart against some mad buggers
Wall

PINK FLOYD THE WALL

In the Flesh?	26
The Thin Ice	28
Another Brick in the Wall. part 1.	30
The Happiest Days of our Lives	35
Another Brick in the Wall. part 2.	37
Mother	40
Goodbye Blue Sky	46
Empty Spaces; / What shall we do now?	49
Young Lust	51
One of my turns	55
Don't Leave me now	59
Another Brick in the Wall. part 3	61
Goodbye Cruel World	63
Hey you	64
Is there anybody out there?	69
Nobody Home	72
Vera	76
Bring the boys back home	78
Comfortably Numb	79
The Show must go on.	84
In the Flesh	86
Run like Hell.	90
Waiting for the worms.	93
Stop	97
The Trial	98
Outside the Wall	103

In the Flesh?

Words & Music by
ROGER WATERS

So ya Thought ya Might like to go to the show ——— To feel ——— the warm ——— thrill of con - fu - sion That

space ca-det glow. ——— Tell me is some-thing e-lud-ing you sun-shine?

Is this not what you ex-pect-ed to see? If you want to find out what's be-hind these cold eyes, You'll

just have to claw your way through this dis-guise. ———

rall. - - -

The Thin Ice

Words & Music by
ROGER WATERS

Another Brick in the Wall, part 1.

Words & Music by
ROGER WATERS

wall.

All in all—

— it was all just bricks in the wall.

The Happiest Days of our Lives

Words & Music by
ROGER WATERS

pour-ing their de-ri-sion——Up-on an-y-thing— we did —— Ex - pos-ing ev -'ry weak-ness How-

ev - er care— ful-ly hid-den by the kids.

But in— the town it was well known When they got

home at night Their fat and psy - cho - path-ic wives would thrash them—With-in inch-es of their lives.

Another Brick in the Wall. part 2.

Words and Music by
ROGER WATERS

fade — — — — — — — — — — — — silence

Mother

Words & Music by
ROGER WATERS

Moth-er, do you think they'll drop— the bomb?

Moth-er, do you think they'll like — the song?

Goodbye Blue Sky

Words & Music by
ROGER WATERS

Empty Spaces / What shall we do now?

Words & Music by
ROGER WATERS

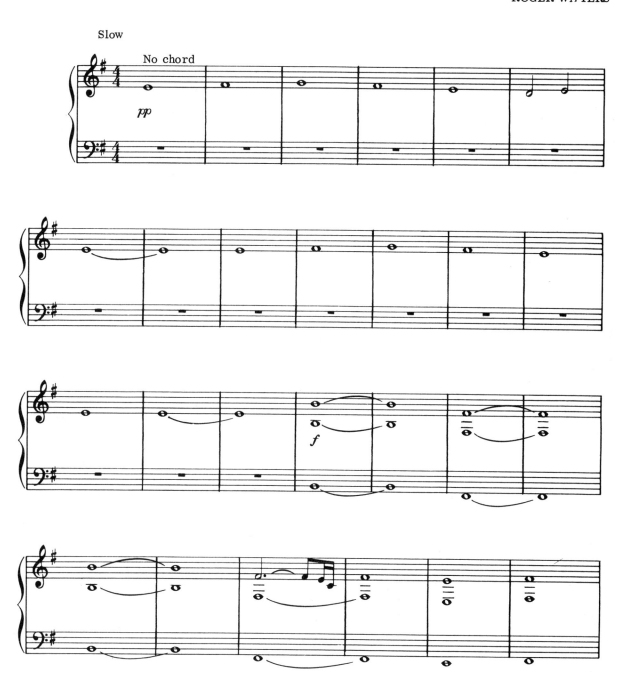

What shall we use — to fill — the emp-ty —

spa - ces — Where — we used to talk? —

How shall I fill the fi-nal — pla - ces?

How should I — com - plete the wall? —

Young Lust

Words & Music by
ROGER WATERS
& DAVID GILMOUR

I am just a new boy, A stran-ger in this town.

Where are all the good times?

Who's gon-na show this stran-ger a - round.

Words & Music by
ROGER WATERS

Would you like to call— the cops? — Do you think it's time— I stopped—

Why are you run-ning a-way?——

Don't Leave me now

Words & Music by
ROGER WATERS

Another Brick in the Wall. part 3.

Words & Music by
ROGER WATERS

I don't need no arms a-round—me.

And I don't need no drugs to calm—me

I have seen the writ-ing on the wall—

Don't think I — need

Goodbye Cruel World

Words & Music by
ROGER WATERS

Slowly

Good-bye, cruel world, I'm leav-ing you to-day. — Good - bye, — Good-bye, — Good - bye.

Good-bye, all you peo-ple, — There's noth-ing you can say To make me change my mind. — Good - bye.

Hey you

Words & Music by
ROGER WATERS

Is there anybody out there?

Words and Music by
ROGER WATERS

Nobody Home

Words and Music by
ROGER WATERS

Vera

Words and Music by
ROGER WATERS

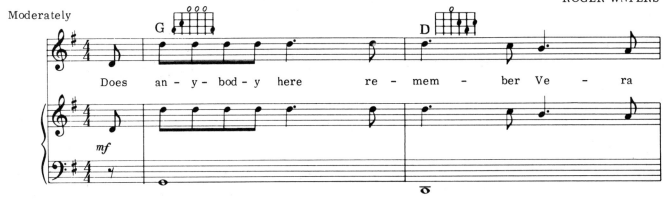

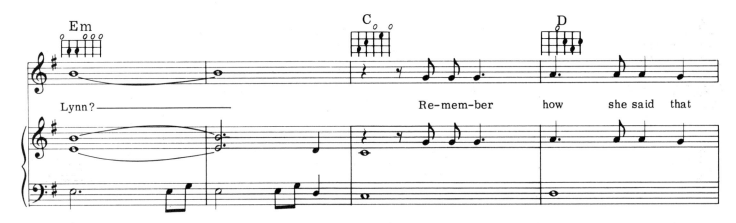

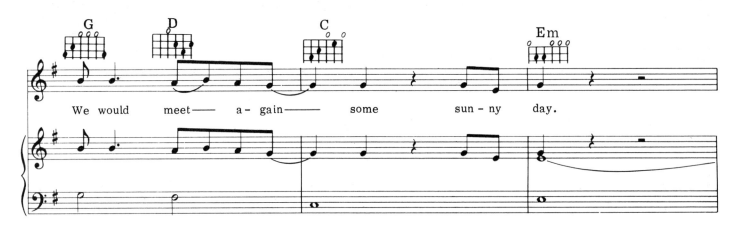

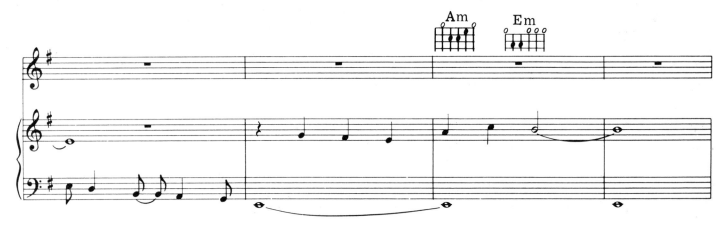

Bring the boys back home

Words and Music by
ROGER WATERS

Comfortably Numb

Words and Music by
DAVID GILMOUR
and ROGER WATERS

83

The Show must go on.

Words and Music by
ROGER WATERS

In the Flesh

Words and Music by
ROGER WATERS

88

Run like Hell.

Words & Music by
DAVID GILMOUR
& ROGER WATERS

Run, run, run, run, run, run,

down your door, — you bet - ter run.
card-board box, — you bet - ter run.

Waiting for the Worms.

Words & Music by
ROGER WATERS

Would you like to see — Bri - tan-nia rule — a - gain — my

friend? All you have to do is fol-low — the worms.

Would you like to send our

col-oured cou-sins home a - gain,— my friend?

Repeat and fade

All you need to do is fol-low— the worms.

Words & Music by
ROGER WATERS

Stop! I wan-na go home, Take off this un-i-form— and

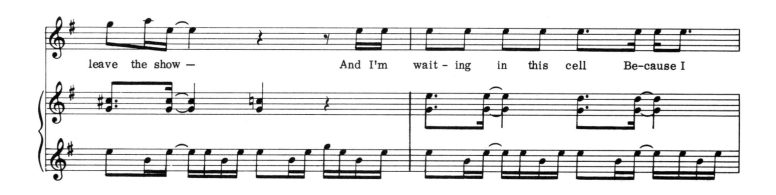

leave the show — And I'm wait-ing in this cell Be-cause I

have to know — Have I — been guil-ty all this

time?

The Trial

Words & Music by
ROGER WATERS
& BOB EZRAM

some-one more de-ser-ving— the full pen-al-ty of law. The way you made them suf-fer, your ex -

quis-ite wife and moth-er, Fills me with the urge to de-fec - ate.

Since, my friend, you have re - vealed your deep-est fear, I sen-tence you to be ex-posed be-

fore your peers. Tear down the wall!

Repeat and fade

8va basso ---------------------------- loco

Outside the Wall

Words & Music by
ROGER WATERS

**Published by Pink Floyd Music Publishers Ltd.,
27 Noel Street, London W1V 3RD.**

Order No. AM 64205
US ISBN 0 8256 1076 1
UK ISBN 0 7119 1031 6

Exclusive Distributors:
Music Sales Corporation
257 Park Avenue South, New York, NY 10010 USA
Music Sales Limited
8/9 Frith Street, London W1V 5TZ England
Music Sales Pty. Limited
120 Rothschild Street, Rosebery, Sydney, NSW 2018, Australia

Printed in the United States of America by
Vicks Lithograph and Printing Corporation